When things feel big,
or dark, or tough,
Being brave means trying stuff.
You might be scared
and that's okay!
Keep on trying every day.

Written & Illustrated by Hein Visser ©2025

All rights reserved. No part of this book may be reproduced, stored in a retrieval system, or transmitted in any form or by any means electronic, mechanical, photocopying, recording, or otherwise without prior written permission from the publisher.

This book is a work of fiction. Any resemblance to actual persons, places, or events is purely coincidental.

For permissions or inquiries, contact:
info@heinvisser.com
Heinvisser.com

A Catalogue record of this book is available from the National Library of New Zealand.

ISBN 978-0-473-75758-8 (paperback)

978-0-473-75759-5 (hardback)

e-book available

Under the floor
of an old farmhouse,
lived four brothers
and a sister mouse.

Her name was Lily,
so small and bright,
adventure was calling,
just out of her sight.

Life was dull
beneath that floor,
so Lily longed
to see much more.

She dreamed of ways to see new places, with magical things and strange new faces.

One dark night
when all were asleep,
Lily crept out,
not making a peep.

She slid down the stairs,
Wheeeee... what a ride,
down to the cellar,
where secrets hide.

Wheeeeeeeee

Down in the cellar,
she saw something new.
A sparkling thing,
shiny like dew.

Just a quick peek,
she thought to herself,
creeping along
the old dusty shelf.

The shiny white threads
felt a little yuck,
and suddenly,
her hand was stuck.

She pulled and pulled,
with all her might,
but the sticky spider web
held her tight.

Down came a spider from way up high, and seeing the mouse, said...

"My, oh my"

"Could this be
a little wee mouse?".

"A tasty little nugget
right here in my house?".

The spider was scary, enormous in size,
it watched her closely with big blue eyes.

Lily had to try and get herself free,
but she was scared, as scared as can be.

Lily just knew
she had to fight,
or it would be
her very last night.

Never give up,
her dad always said,
never, ever listen
to the voice of dread.

Always be brave,
your head held high,
and don't be scared
to try, try, try.

Good evening Mr. Spider",
Lily said so polite,
"Isn't it lovely
this calm, starry night?"

"To me, you look
handsome as can be,
but you wouldn't like
a little mouse like me".

GR

The spider was hungry and didn't hear a thing, just thought of the joy this nugget would bring.

He started dreaming of dishes and treats, and each scrumptious thought was oh-so-sweet.

RRRRRRRRr

"Maybe I'll have you with beans on toast, for that's the taste I love the most".

"Maybe I'll cook you slow in a pot. I really like that thought a lot".

"Hmmm, Maybe I'll have you,
with crackers and tea.
That sounds oh so Yummy to me".

The spider just didn't know what to think
when Lily gave him a cheeky wink.

"Doesn't each mouse get one last wish,
before she becomes a spider's dish?"

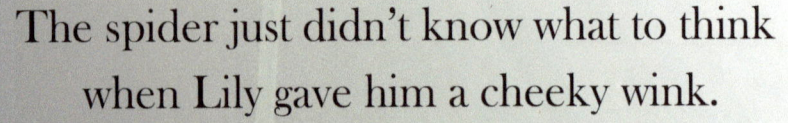

The spider had a think, and said: "I agree.
So, tell me little mouse, what will it be?"

Lily started speaking, not sure of herself.
She had to try something, alone on that shelf.

"In the cellar, there's a small piece of cheese.
May I have it? Pretty, pretty please?"

"Even a small piece of cheese like that,
will surely make me juicy and fat.

"I'll be so soft and lovely to chew;
juicy and tender, good for a stew."

"Then," said the spider,
"Let it be so;
down to the cellar,
I shall go."

He slipped up the web
as quiet as he came,
with finding that cheese
his only aim.

...that was the sound
of a wooden mouse trap

Lily's mom always warned,
"Stay clear of that trap,
'cause that's how we lost
our dear Uncle Chap."

With two big teeth,
as sharp as swords,
Lily bit fast
and chewed through the cords.

As fast as lightning,
quick as a flash.
She darted upstairs,
in a single dash!

Lily had a thought
before she fell asleep,
before she counted
Lalaland sheep.

When she was stuck,
all alone on that shelf.
She didn't give up
and believed in herself.

She tried her plan
and saw it through.
Cause that's the thing
that brave kids do.

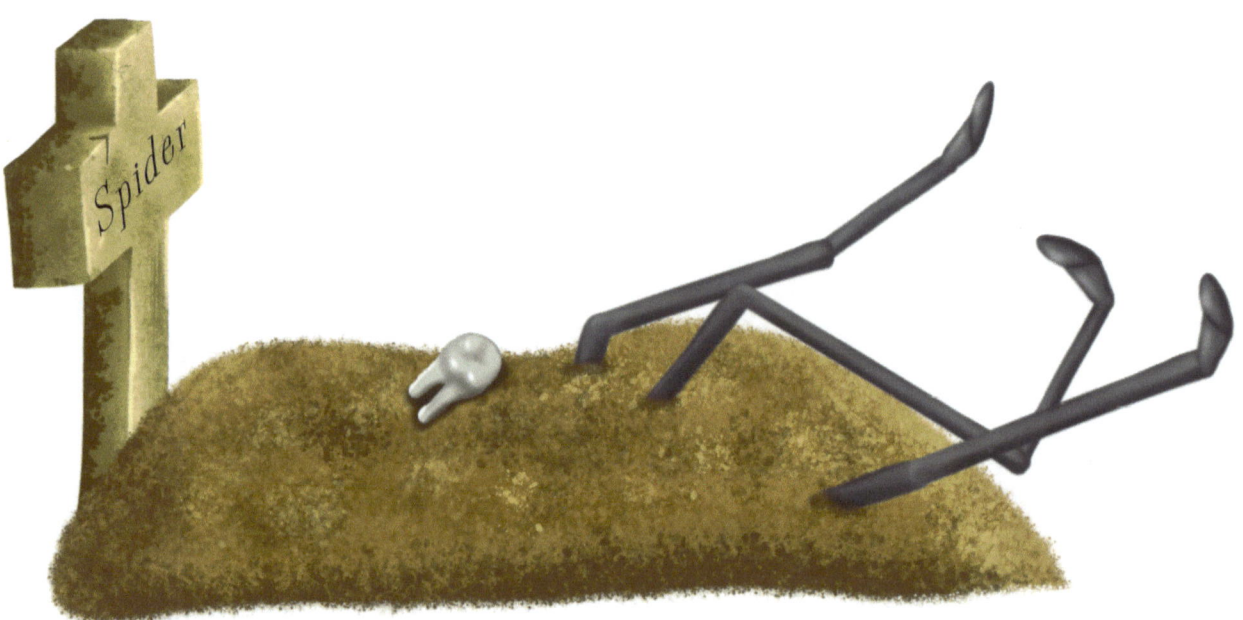

When things feel big,
or dark, or tough,
Being brave means trying stuff.
You might be scared
and that's okay!
Keep on trying every day.